Milton Hershey

History Maker Bios

Jane Sutcliffe

LERNER PUBLICATIONS COMPANY • MINNEAPOLIS

For the sweet things in my life: Skip, John, and Michael

Special thanks to Pamela Whitenack, Hershey Community Archives

Illustrations by Tim Parlin

Lerner Publications Company
A division of Lerner Publishing Group
241 First Avenue North
Minneapolis, MN 55401 U.S.A.

Website address: www.lernerbooks.com

Library of Congress Cataloging-in-Publication Data

Sutcliffe, Jane.
    Milton Hershey / by Jane Sutcliffe.
        p.   cm. — (History maker bios)
    Summary: A biography of the successful chocolate maker who built a town around his factory with unique housing for his workers and a school for disadvantaged students.
    Includes bibliographical references and index.
    ISBN: 0–8225–0247–X (lib. bdg. : alk. paper)
    1. Hershey, Milton Snavely, 1857–1945—Juvenile literature.
    2. Businessmen—United States—Biography—Juvenile literature. 3. Hershey Foods Corporation—History—Juvenile literature. 4. Chocolate industry—United States—History—Juvenile literature. [1. Hershey, Milton Snavely, 1857–1945. 2. Confectioners. 3. Businessmen.] I. Title. II. Series.
    HD9200.U52 H4763 2004
    338.7'664153'092—dc21   2002015766

Manufactured in the United States of America
1 2 3 4 5 6 – JR – 09 08 07 06 05 04

TABLE OF CONTENTS

INTRODUCTION

Nearly everyone knows the name Hershey. That's because Milton Hershey put his name on one of the most delicious foods in the world—chocolate. In the early 1900s, he invented a new recipe for milk chocolate. His five-cent chocolate bars became a big business.

But Milton Hershey wasn't always successful. The first few times he tried to sell candy, he failed. Still, Milton would not give up. He worked hard to invent delicious new recipes. He kept trying until his candy made him a wealthy man. Then he surprised everyone by giving his money away.

This is his story.

1 Candy Maker

Imagine growing up in a land without chocolate. Milton Hershey did. When he was born in 1857, chocolate candy was still a new invention in Europe. Shops in the United States didn't even sell it yet. Milton could spend his pennies on peppermints, taffy, and sourballs. But he would have to wait many years for his first delicious bite of chocolate.

Milton was born in a stone farmhouse in Derry Township, Pennsylvania. Most people in Derry Township belonged to the Mennonite religion. So did Milton's family. Mennonites dressed plainly and worked hard as farmers. They didn't go to dances or play cards. They didn't even read books for fun.

As a boy, Milton's favorite candies were sourballs. They were so big they made his cheeks bulge.

People called Milton's father, Henry Hershey, a dreamer.

But Milton's father, Henry, did some odd things for a Mennonite. He loved to read books. He enjoyed learning about anything new—new machines, new crops, or new breeds of farm animals. Henry was always dreaming of new ways to get rich, too. None of his big ideas ever worked out.

Milton's mother, Fanny, didn't believe in big ideas. She believed in hard work. So Milton learned to work hard on the Hersheys' farm. He got up early to lead the cows to pasture and to feed the chickens.

But Milton was like his father, too. He knew he could never be happy as a simple farmer. He was always wondering what lay beyond their farm.

When Milton was growing up, boys often left school early to learn a job. That's what Milton did. At thirteen, he got a job learning to run a printing press.

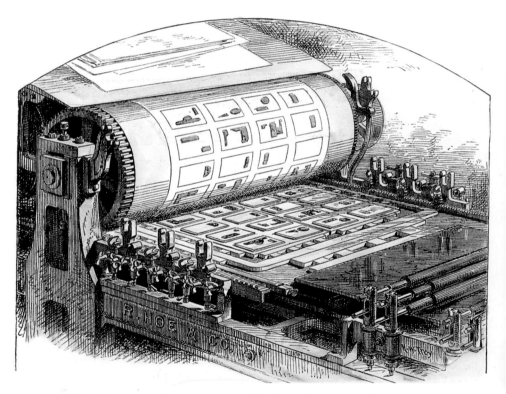

Milton's new job was to set blocks of type on a printing press. Each block had to be set by hand.

Poor Milton hated his job. He was clumsy. When he dropped things, his boss exploded in anger. After one scolding, Milton dropped his straw hat into the press "accidentally on purpose," as he explained later. The press jammed, and Milton was fired.

Fanny knew that printing was not the job for her son. She found him a job at Joseph Royer's ice cream and candy shop in Lancaster, Pennsylvania. Milton was overjoyed. Making candy sounded like much more fun than working at the printing press.

Milton was right. Making candy was fun. And to his surprise, he found he had a talent for it. Mr. Royer didn't write down his recipes. Milton simply added a little of this or a little of that to the mix. He learned just which ingredients would make taffy, peppermints, or caramels taste better. Milton's candy became very popular.

After four years at Mr. Royer's shop, Milton had become a young man. He was short and solid, with blue eyes and thick eyebrows. His voice was soft and gentle.

AN EXPLOSIVE MISTAKE

Milton made his share of mistakes while he was working at Royer's. Once he forgot that he had been roasting peanuts. He left for the day without turning off the hot-air blower that roasted the nuts. Later that evening, he went to a play in the theater next door. He smelled burning peanuts and ran back to the shop. Burned peanut shells were blowing around like dry leaves!

Milton had learned all he could from Mr. Royer. He decided it was time to start his own candy business. The year was 1876. The United States was celebrating its one-hundredth birthday. Much of the birthday celebration was taking place in the city of Philadelphia, Pennsylvania. Thousands of people were crowding into the city for the fun. Philadelphia would be the place to sell his candy, Milton decided.

He borrowed $150 from his mother's sister, Mattie, to buy equipment. His uncle, Abe, helped him move. At nineteen, Milton was on his way to Philadelphia.

2 TRY, TRY AGAIN

The sweet smell of candy filled
Milton's shop on Spring Garden
Street. Milton sold each piece of his candy
for a penny. But candy was made with
sugar, and sugar was expensive. He had to
sell lots of candy just to pay for the sugar.

Milton worked hard, just as he had back on the farm. His mother and Aunt Mattie came to Philadelphia to help. Still, there always seemed to be more money going out of the shop than coming in.

Again and again, Aunt Mattie wrote to Uncle Abe to ask for more money. It was never enough. Finally, after six years, Milton locked the doors of his shop for the last time.

Milton wasn't ready to give up on making candy. He found a job with another candy maker in Denver, Colorado. This man made delicious caramels with fresh milk.

Milton had cards printed to tell people about his business. This one showed a famous building in Philadelphia.

M. S. HERSHEY
DEALER IN

FINE CONFECTIONERY, FRUITS, NUTS, &c.

No. 935 SPRING GARDEN STREET,   PHILADELPHIA.

Milton liked his job. But he still dreamed of running his own business. So after a few months, he went to Chicago, then to New Orleans, then to New York. In each place, Milton tried making and selling candy. In each place, he failed. He couldn't make enough money to pay his bills.

By 1886, Milton had just enough money left for a train ticket home to Lancaster. He knocked on Uncle Abe's door. But Uncle Abe didn't want anything to do with Milton. He thought he had spent enough money on Milton's dreams.

BAD LUCK WITH A HORSE

In New York, Milton sold cough drops as well as candy. One day, some boys tossed firecrackers under his horse. Terrified, it raced wildly down the street. Milton chased the poor animal, but he never did catch it. "You could trace the way it went by the cough drops scattered in the street," he told his mother.

Aunt Mattie helped Milton with his new caramel business. One of her jobs was wrapping candies in tinfoil.

Even his family thought he was a failure! No one would have blamed Milton if he had quit the candy business then and there. But he refused to give up.

A friend gave Milton a place to stay and enough money to start his candy business one more time. Milton remembered the good caramels he had made in Denver. So this time, he decided to sell caramels made with fresh milk. He called his new business the Lancaster Caramel Company.

Milton sold his candy from a cart he pushed around town himself. People liked Milton's caramels. Still, he dreamed of making his business bigger. But he had no money to do that.

Then one day, a traveler from England came to Lancaster and bought some of Milton's caramels. He had never tasted anything like them! The man wanted to sell the caramels in England. He placed a huge order.

Fresh milk became the secret to the Lancaster Caramel Company's success.

Milton knew that this order was the break he needed. But to make so many caramels, he needed more equipment and supplies. A banker named Mr. Brenneman agreed to loan Milton $700. Milton would have to pay back the loan in ninety days.

Milton hired more workers. He added more equipment. He worked hard to make all the caramels for the English buyer. In fact, he was still hard at work when the ninety days were up. Milton had to tell Mr. Brenneman that he could not repay the loan. Even worse, he needed still more money for supplies.

Besides fresh milk, Milton's caramels were made with cream, sugar, and corn syrup.

Mr. Brenneman knew he should say no. His bosses at the bank would never approve the loan. But Mr. Brenneman liked Milton. So he did something that was against the rules. He put his own name on the loan instead of Milton's. He would have to pay back the loan if Milton could not.

The extra money was enough for Milton to fill the order. He kept making and selling caramels. He was eager to repay Mr. Brenneman's kindness—and the loan. As soon as his payment arrived from England, he raced to the bank. The people of Lancaster must have chuckled when they saw him. Milton hadn't even stopped to take off his candy-spattered apron!

That was an important day for Milton Hershey. Suddenly, after so many failures, it looked like he would be a success after all.

3 SWEET SUCCESS

The order from England was just the beginning. Soon people all over the world were eating Milton's caramels. All those caramels made thirty-three-year-old Milton a rich man.

Milton had fun experimenting with new kinds of caramels. He made some with rich cream. He put icing on others. Still others had fancy shapes. His workers thought it was funny to see their boss with his sleeves rolled up, trying out some new recipe. He never approved a recipe until the flavor was just right. Milton wanted his caramels to be the best anyone had ever tasted.

By age thirty-five, Milton was one of Lancaster's richest citizens.

Milton saw many new inventions and machines during his trip to Chicago in 1893.

He liked thinking up unusual names for the new candies, too. There were Roly Polies, McGinties, Jim Cracks, and Lotuses. Sometimes he held a contest among his workers. The one who thought up the best name won.

Just like his father, Milton loved new inventions and new ideas. In 1893, a huge world's fair was held in Chicago. The fair showed off inventions from all over the world. Milton was fascinated by some machinery from Germany. The machinery turned cocoa beans and sugar into chocolate.

Milton made chocolates in many shapes. This candy looked like a fan.

For the first time, Milton smelled that wonderful chocolate smell. He tasted the delicious flavor. A new candy—that was just the kind of thing that excited Milton! He made up his mind at once. "I'm going to make chocolate," he said. He bought the machinery then and there.

Soon Milton's factory was turning out dark, sweet chocolates. Milton made them in all kinds of shapes—114 of them! A customer who wanted a chocolate shaped like a bicycle, a cigar, or a lobster could find it at the Hershey Chocolate Company.

Kitty was twenty-six years old when she and Milton married.

Milton liked to visit the shops where his candy was sold. At a candy store in New York, he met a salesgirl named Catherine Sweeney. Milton called her Kitty. Kitty was young and beautiful. She had a lively sense of humor, too.

Milton began to visit Kitty often. Soon they fell in love. On May 25, 1898, they were married. Milton brought Kitty home to his big, comfortable house in Lancaster.

Milton began to think more and more about chocolate. He was already one of the first chocolate makers in the country. He wanted to be the biggest.

In August of 1900, Milton made an important decision. He sold the Lancaster Caramel Company. The headlines in that day's paper told the story: CARAMEL FACTORY SOLD. MILTON S. HERSHEY RECEIVES A MILLION DOLLARS FOR IT.

The sign for the Lancaster Caramel Company was taken down. But Milton still had the chocolate company. And he had big plans. Best of all, he had the money to put his plans into action.

A TITANIC BIT OF LUCK

Milton and Kitty loved to travel. They took many trips to Europe. Once they bought tickets for a trip on a magnificent new ship. But at the last minute, their plans changed. It was a good thing, too. The ship was the *Titanic*. It sank on its first ocean voyage!

4 A FACTORY IN A CORNFIELD

Milton's new ideas seemed to come tumbling out of him one after another. First he decided he wanted to make milk chocolate. No one else in the United States made milk chocolate. Milton would be the first.

Up to this point, Milton's company had only made dark, sweet chocolate. Milk chocolate was smoother and creamier. It was also much harder to make. Milton was not a scientist. He had always invented new candies just by trying to see what worked. That's what he did now.

Things did not go well at first. Milton threw out batch after batch of ruined chocolate. But when something went right, his workers would hear him shout, "We've got it!" Bit by bit, Milton came up with his own recipe for milk chocolate. In 1900, he started making Hershey's Milk Chocolate Bars. They were an instant success.

Hershey bars have been a favorite treat for more than one hundred years.

The farmers in Derry Township raised many cows. Milton knew he would have the milk he needed to make milk chocolate.

It was time for Milton to put his next idea into action. He wanted to build a bigger factory. He knew just where he wanted to put it—in Derry Township, where he had been born. There was plenty of land and clean water there. There was a railroad to ship his chocolate to customers. Best of all, there were plenty of cows. They would supply the milk he needed to make milk chocolate.

Most people thought he was crazy when they heard his plan. Factories weren't built in the middle of a cornfield, everyone said. They were built in towns. A factory needed people. People needed houses. They needed schools and churches.

But Milton had one more big idea. He would build not only a factory. He would build a town around it.

In 1903, work began on the factory. It was as big as two football fields. Inside, there was room for six hundred workers.

Milton spread the word about his business with this electric car.

As the factory went up, the town spread out. Milton planned the neighborhoods. He named the main streets Chocolate Avenue and Cocoa Avenue. Other streets were named for places where cocoa beans came from, like Java, Caracas, and Trinidad.

Most factory towns had houses that all looked alike. Houses were cheaper to build that way. That wasn't good enough for Milton. He wanted each home to have its own style. Once he found that a builder had made too many houses that looked the same. Milton ordered all the houses torn down. Then they were rebuilt his way.

Milton picked the names for his town's streets himself.

FORGET THE BROCCOLI—EAT YOUR CHOCOLATE!
Milton kept making chocolate in Lancaster while
his new factory was being built. He didn't allow
his workers to call his chocolate "candy." He
thought of it as a healthy, nutritious food.
Magazine and newspaper ads even called a
chocolate bar "a meal in itself."

He wanted the
houses to be as
up-to-date as possible,

too. Instead of outhouses, the new homes
had indoor toilets. Instead of being crowded
together close to the street, they had pretty
lawns and big backyards. Making the
houses so fancy cost Milton extra money.
But he didn't mind. He just wanted his
workers and their families to be happy.

Milton set up trolley lines so people
could easily visit his town from other
places. He built schools and churches.
There were stores, an inn, and a bank.

Milton invited the workers from his old factory to work at the new one. That way, no one lost a job because of the move.

Milton wanted the townspeople to have fun. So he built a park, golf courses, and a zoo. He started a fire department and even became a volunteer firefighter.

Milton's town had everything but a post office. To get one, the town needed a name. So a contest was held to name the town. The winning entry was Hersheykoko. The United States postmaster had to approve the name, though, and he didn't like it. The name was shortened, and the town became just Hershey.

Milton's chocolate factory was ready to run in 1905. Visitors came to marvel at the giant machines grinding and mixing away. They stared at the enormous vats of liquid chocolate. They breathed in the delicious smell of chocolate. Soon that smell filled the town.

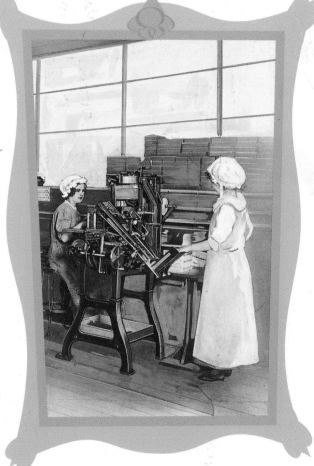

Making milk chocolate was a hard job. But Milton's workers could eat all the chocolate they wanted.

Milton decided that he wouldn't make 114 kinds of chocolates anymore. He would make only a few. His Hershey's Milk Chocolate Bars were already big sellers. In 1907, Milton started making Hershey's Kisses. These were little bell-shaped milk chocolates wrapped in silver foil. They became just as popular as Milton's chocolate bars.

Hershey's Kisses became so popular that the town of Hershey put in streetlights shaped like them.

With only a few products to make, Milton's huge factory could produce lots and lots of chocolates. The more chocolates he made, the more cheaply he could sell them. And the cheaper the price, the more chocolates Milton sold. Nearly everyone could afford to buy a chocolate bar that cost a nickel.

Milton wanted everyone to see and buy his candy. He sold his chocolates not just in candy shops. He sold them in grocery stores, at bus stops, and at newsstands all over the country. No one had done that before. Soon Hershey's Kisses and Hershey's Milk Chocolate Bars were everywhere.

And, of course, so was Milton's name. Before long, the name Hershey meant chocolate to most people.

5 KITTY'S IDEA

By 1909, Milton and Kitty had more money than they had ever dreamed possible. They wanted to do something special with it. This time, it was Kitty who had a big idea. She and Milton had no children of their own. Why not start a home and school for children whose parents had died or could not care for them?

Milton loved Kitty's idea. Soon two brothers became the first students of the Hershey Industrial School. The boys lived in the Hershey Homestead—the same stone farmhouse where Milton had been born. They went to classes and did chores. They milked cows and fed chickens, just as Milton had done when he was a boy.

Milton and Kitty's school grew quickly. Milton loved to visit the students. He made sure they had everything they needed. He was as proud of them as any father.

The Hershey Homestead made a good home for the first students at Milton's school.

This photo of Milton and Kitty was taken shortly before she became ill.

Kitty wasn't able to visit the school, though. She was very ill. Milton took her to doctors and clinics around the world. She only got weaker. In 1915, she died.

Milton was heartbroken. He missed Kitty terribly. He decided to do something extraordinary in her honor. Milton and Kitty had already given a good deal of money to the school. In 1918, when he was sixty-one, Milton gave his whole fortune—all sixty million dollars—to the school. Other wealthy people gave money to charities, too. But no one gave *everything* away.

Milton didn't want people making a big fuss about his gift. He made no speech or announcement. He didn't tell newspaper reporters about it. Years passed before the public found out what Milton had done. That was fine with him. He was happy just knowing that Kitty would have been proud.

Milton always loved to spend Sundays with the students at his school.

In the early 1920s, business boomed in Hershey. The factory turned out millions of dollars worth of chocolates every year. Then, in 1929, hard times came to the whole country. People called these times the Great Depression. Workers lost their jobs. Many people went hungry.

Milton did not want these things to happen in Hershey. He planned all kinds of new building projects to make sure all the workers in town had jobs.

The Great Depression left many families without jobs and homes.

The government created new jobs by paying for building projects. Milton did the same thing for the people of Hershey.

A YOUNG MAN'S OPPORTUNITY

CCC

FOR WORK PLAY STUDY & HEALTH

APPLICATIONS TAKEN BY
ILLINOIS EMERGENCY RELIEF COMMISSION
ILLINOIS SELECTING AGENCY

Some people told Milton he was crazy. He should be saving the company's money, not spending it on new buildings, they said.

Milton didn't care what people thought. Once someone pointed out a steam shovel at one of his building sites. The steam shovels did the work of forty men, the builder said proudly. Milton was horrified. "Take them off," he said. "Hire forty men."

By 1936, the worst of the Great Depression was over. Milton was proud that no workers in Hershey had lost their jobs.

41

By now, Milton was an old man. In 1937, when he was eighty, visitors from the United States Army came to see him. They thought a war might be coming, and they wanted their soldiers to be prepared. They asked Milton to make a new kind of chocolate bar. The bar would be an emergency food supply for soldiers.

Milton and his staff worked hard to create the Field Ration D bar. They put in extra vitamins and other healthy ingredients. Eating three of the bars was like eating a whole day's meals. Best of all, the bars didn't melt in a soldier's pocket. American soldiers and sailors ate Field Ration D bars all through World War II.

DESSERT, ANYONE?

Milton never lost his love for experimenting with new things. As an old man, he tried new recipes for unusual frozen desserts. His potato ice cream and beet sherbet never quite caught on!

Milton celebrated his eighty-eighth birthday with cake and a party.

Milton lived just long enough to see the end of the war. He died on October 13, 1945. He was eighty-eight. During his life, he started one of the nation's most successful businesses. He built a thriving town. He made chocolate the country's favorite treat. These were his gifts to the world. But he was always most proud of his school and of the children he had helped. They were his gift to the future.

TIMELINE

In the year . . .

1871   he got a job running a printing press.

1872   he got a job as a candy maker.   Age 15

1876   he started his own candy business.

1882   his business failed.

1886   he started his fifth candy business.

1890   his caramel business made him rich.   Age 33

1894   he started to make chocolate.

1898   he married Kitty Sweeney.

1900   he sold his caramel company for one million dollars.   Age 42

     he started to make Hershey's Milk Chocolate Bars.

1903   work started on his new factory and the town of Hershey, Pennsylvania.

1905   his new factory opened.

1907   he started to make Hershey's Kisses.

1909   he opened the Hershey Industrial School.   Age 52

1915   Kitty died.

1918   he gave his whole fortune to the Hershey Industrial School.

1937   he started work on the Field Ration D bar for soldiers.

1945   he died on October 13.   Age 88

THE MILTON HERSHEY SCHOOL

The gift of Milton's fortune made sure that his school would help children for years to come. The Hershey Industrial School has been renamed the Milton Hershey School. Nearly 1,200 boys and girls live and study there at no charge. The school gives the students everything they need, from backpacks to braces.

Milton never dreamed how large his school would grow. He once said, "If we helped a hundred children, it would have been all worthwhile." Since 1909, Milton's school has helped thousands. It is the biggest American school that offers a home to its students.

And it all began with chocolate.

FURTHER READING

NONFICTION
**Burleigh, Robert. *Chocolate: Riches from the Rainforest.*
New York: Harry N. Abrams, Inc., 2002.** The colorful story
of chocolate, including its history and uses throughout
world history.

**Palotta, Jerry. *The Hershey's Milk Chocolate Bar
Fractions Book.* New York: Scholastic, 1999.** You can do
more with a Hershey bar than just eat it—you can also use
its twelve sections to practice fractions.

**Raven, Margot Theis. *Mercedes and the Chocolate Pilot.*
Chelsea, MI: Sleeping Bear Press, 2002.** The true story of a
pilot who dropped gifts of chocolate as he flew over the city
of Berlin during the years after World War II.

FICTION
**Catling, Patrick Skene. *The Chocolate Touch.* New York:
William Morrow & Co., 1979.** Young John Midas discovers
that everything he touches turns to chocolate—and he isn't
sure he's happy about it!

**Dahl, Roald. *Charlie and the Chocolate Factory.* New
York: Knopf, 1964.** A poor boy named Charlie Bucket goes
on an amazing adventure in Willy Wonka's chocolate
factory in this beloved children's classic.

WEBSITES

Hershey's Kidztown
<http://www.kidztown.com/> Play games, try out recipes,
and take a tour of the Hershey factory at this fun website.

MiltonHershey.com
<http://www.miltonhershey.com> Visitors to this site can view a biography and photos of Milton and learn about the Milton Hershey School.

SELECT BIBLIOGRAPHY

Brenner, Joel Glenn. *The Emperors of Chocolate: Inside the Secret World of Hershey and Mars*. New York: Random House, 1999.

Castner, Charles Schuyler. *One of a Kind*. Hershey, PA: The Derry Literary Guild, 1983.

Coe, Sophie D. and Michael D. Coe. *The True History of Chocolate*. New York: Thames and Hudson, 1996.

Malone, Mary. *Milton Hershey: Chocolate King*. Champaign, IL: Garrard Publishing Company, 1971.

Morton, Marcia and Frederic Morton. *Chocolate: An Illustrated History*. New York: Crown Publishers, Inc., 1986.

Shippen, Katherine B. and Paul A. W. Wallace. *Milton S. Hershey*. New York: Random House, 1959.

Snavely, Joseph Richard. *An Intimate Story of Milton S. Hershey*. Hershey, PA: Hershey Chocolate Corporation, 1957.

Wallace, Paul A. W. *Milton S. Hershey*. Privately printed, 1955.

INDEX

Acknowledgments

For photographs and artwork: Hershey Community Archives, pp. 4, 7, 8, 10, 14, 16, 21, 23, 24, 29, 30, 31, 32, 33, 38, 39, 43, 45; © North Wind Picture Archive, p. 9; © Todd Strand/Independent Picture Service, pp. 17, 18, 27, 34; Westinghouse Historical Collection, p. 22; Agricultural Research Service, USDA, p. 28; Jane Sutcliffe, p. 37; Franklin D. Roosevelt Library, NLR-PHOCO-A-7182, p. 40; Library of Congress, LC-USZC2-862, p. 41. Front and back cover, Hershey Community Archives.

For quoted material: pp. 11, 27, Wallace, Paul A. W. *Milton S. Hershey*. Privately printed, 1955; p. 15, Shippen, Katherine B. and Paul A. W. Wallace. *Milton S. Hershey*. New York: Random House, 1959; p. 41, Reda, Lou, prod. *Biography: Milton Hershey: The Chocolate King*. A&E Television Networks, 1995. Videocassette; p. 45, Milton Hershey School, March 2002, "Milton Hershey School History," <www.mhs-pa.org/historical/history.html>.